USDA

United States
Department
of Agriculture

CWS-15c-01
March 2015

Outlook

Approved by USDA's
World Agricultural
Outlook Board

A Report from the Economic Research Service

www.ers.usda.gov

I0408611

Cotton Policy in China

Stephen MacDonald, Fred Gale, and James Hansen

Abstract

This report examines China's 2011-13 attempt to maintain a high level of price support for its cotton producers, analyzing the policy's motivation, its consequences to date, and the impacts of various adjustment alternatives China might pursue. With China's wages rising rapidly in recent years, cotton production costs there have been rising faster than in the rest of the world. Rising costs both helped motivate China's policymakers to strengthen their price support for cotton production in 2011 and ensured that the policy ultimately proved unsustainable. After several years of sharply lower cotton consumption and sharply rising state-owned stockpiles of cotton, China in 2014 began switching producer support to direct subsidies, and focusing support on producers in the largest producing region, Xinjiang. Additional reforms include plans to restore market forces to a leading role in determining China's cotton prices. But China's large role in world cotton markets and the unprecedented size of the Government's stocks mean that difficult choices lie ahead for China's policymakers. Policy decisions in China will continue to have a significant impact on the rest of the world, and lower Chinese import quotas for cotton could reduce world cotton prices significantly.

Keywords: Cotton, China, agricultural policy, price supports, trade, textiles, trade policy, WTO, industrial policy

Acknowledgments

The authors would like to thank USDA's Interagency Commodity Estimates Committee (ICEC) for Cotton and the staff of the U.S. Embassy in Beijing. Without their input, much of this report would not have been possible. Discussions with ICEC members helped shape the authors' understanding of China's cotton policy, and data collected for ICEC analysis has been an invaluable resource. Hunter Colby (USDA/World Agricultural Outlook Board), James Johnson (USDA/Foreign Agricultural Service), Leslie Meyer (USDA/ERS), and Carol Skelly (USDA/WAOB) have been valuable resources for China cotton analysis for many years. This report also benefited from reviews by Mark Jekanowski (USDA/ERS), Maurice Landes (USDA/ERS), James Johnson (USDA/FAS), Carol Skelly (USDA/WOAB), Björn Alpermann (Universtät Würburg), John C. Robinson (Texas A&M University), and Scott Sanford (USDA/Farm Service Agency). Thanks also to Priscilla Smith and Cynthia A. Ray of ERS for editorial and design assistance.

Introduction

China's introduction of a temporary cotton stockpiling program during 2011-13 created a price floor that significantly increased support to its farmers, drove cotton textile fiber use out of the country, and resulted in an unprecedented level of ending stocks for China and the world. This movement from China's previous "soft" price support program to a formal, high level of price support proved costly and unsustainable and a shift toward subsidy payments to farmers began in 2014. While China's cotton production likely will fall while consumption of cotton rises, the policy transition also will likely include a reduction in the country's extraordinarily large stocks. The reduction of stocks will lead to some combination of lower prices and production of cotton outside of China, and, given the size of China's cotton industry and stocks, these declines could be large.

Today, cotton's "world" price is the price at ports in and near China. International commodity trading firms store large volumes of cotton in China at their own expense and the Zhengzhou Commodity Exchange's (ZCE) No.1 Cotton futures contract is followed by traders throughout the world, vying with the New York market as a source of market information (Ge, Wang, and Ahn, 2010; Jernigan, 2005). Despite the decades of reform in China that helped make this possible, its cotton supply, demand, and prices are still driven to a large extent by an extensive set of highly variable and somewhat opaque policies.

In many respects, the world cotton market revolves around China, the world's largest consumer, importer, and stockholder of cotton by sizable margins, and the second largest producer (fig. 1). China consistently has been the world's largest importer since 2003, but its impact on world markets was outsized well before then. In the early 1970s, China began appearing in the top ranks of global

Figure 1
China leads world cotton markets

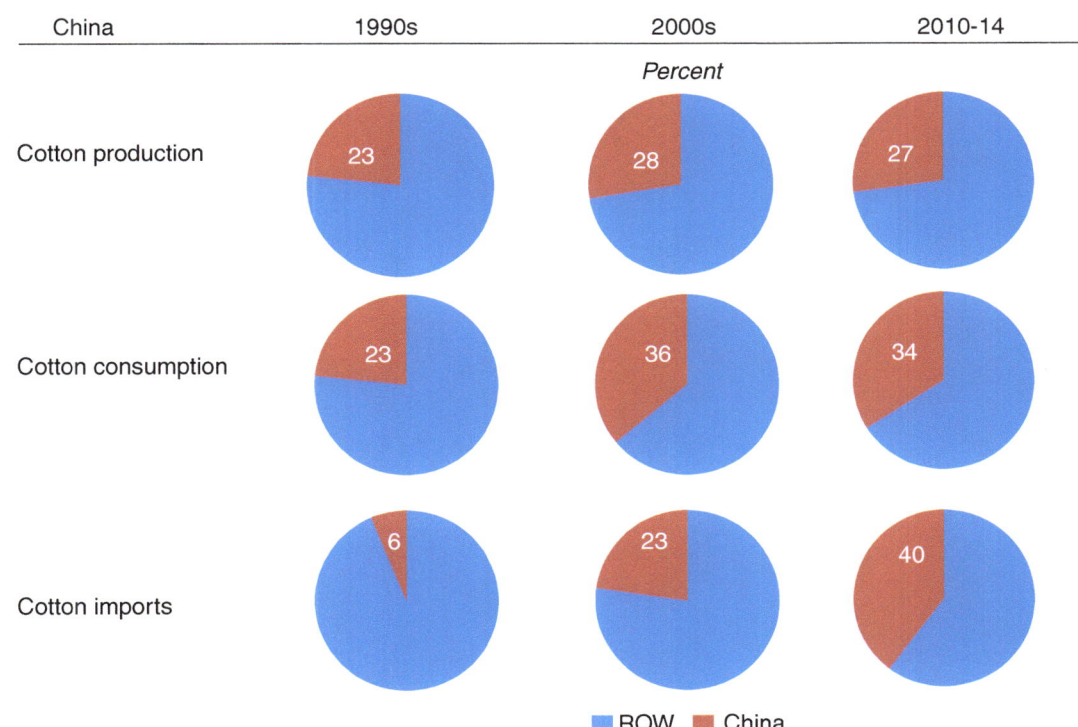

Source: USDA, Economic Research Service based on data from USDA, Foreign Agricultural Service, 2014b.

Cotton Policy in China, CWS-15c-01
Economic Research Service/USDA

importers, and it became the world's largest net importer in 1979. But in subsequent years, China's trade position was highly volatile, including periods as a large net exporter, establishing China as a significant source of uncertainty for the rest of the world, as it is today.

The accumulation of cotton in China's intervention stockpiles since 2011 has introduced a new degree of uncertainty into world cotton markets. Defending a high domestic cotton price during 2011-13, China has driven world cotton stocks to nearly double the average levels—and 45 percent above the previous record—for the years since 1950. With world ending stocks near 90 percent of use in 2012 and 2013, global cotton markets face a difficult and costly transition if policy shifts in China return world stocks to normal levels with anything other than a long period of transition.

Cotton in China Agriculture

As in most countries, cotton's role in China's agriculture is relatively small, accounting for 2 percent to 4 percent of planted area and value of output for agriculture. As is the case for most other field crops in China, farms growing cotton are typically about 0.5 hectare in size, and about half or less of their area farmed is devoted to cotton (1 hectare = 2.47 acres). Out of about 200 million people in China currently employed in primary agriculture, perhaps 100 million participate in the production of cotton (Hua, 2013). But, as is true for other commodities, cotton production is increasingly a part-time occupation for farmers in China. Cotton has steadily accounted for a significant share of China's agricultural imports by value in recent years. At about 10 percent of import value since 2003, cotton's share has been below that of soybeans (about 30 percent), and comparable to vegetable oil (14 percent) and rubber (7 percent), the other large agricultural imports.

One thing that distinguishes cotton from other crops in China is the large share of production concentrated in Xinjiang Uygur Autonomous Region, in the upper northwestern corner of the country (fig 2). Cotton was traditionally grown in eastern China near the Yellow River (in Hebei, Henan, and Shandong provinces) and the Yangtze River (Anhui, Hubei, Hunan, and Jiangsu provinces) (fig 3). But since 2005, Xinjiang has become China's dominant cotton-growing region. Virtually all of the cotton grown in the eastern regions is genetically modified (GM), but only a small share of the cotton grown in Xinjiang is GM cotton. Xinjiang's climate and geography limited the bollworm infestations that drove production costs sharply higher in eastern China during the late 1980s and early 1990s, and the introduction of GM varieties has not been necessary. Since 2010, Xinjiang has accounted for about 50 percent or more of China's cotton output, and is likely to see its share continue to rise.

Figure 2
China cotton production by producing region, 1980-2014

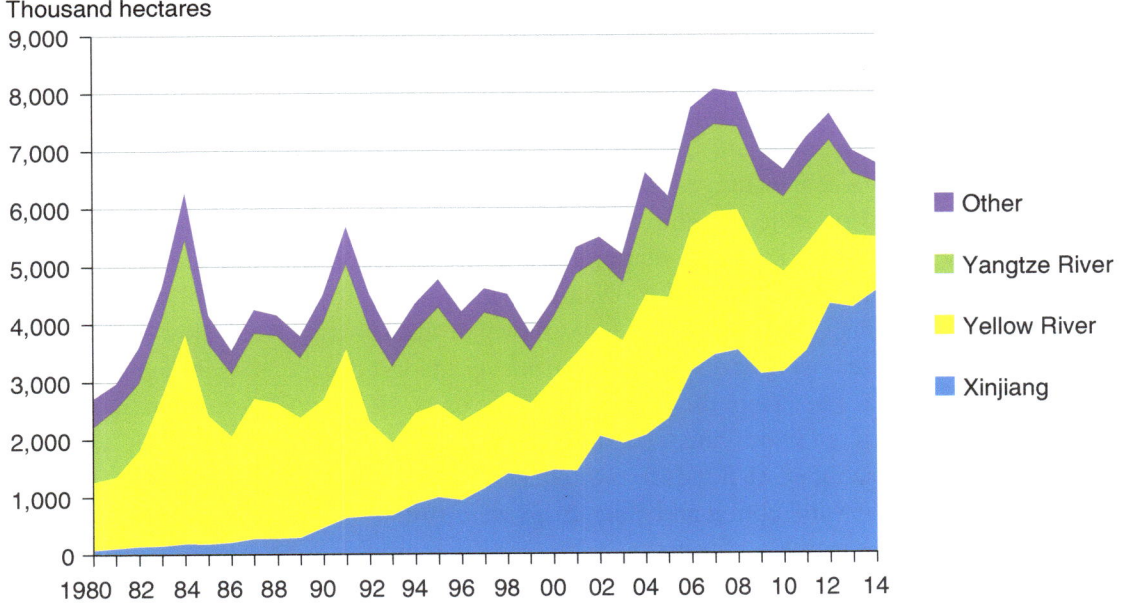

Thousand hectares

Note: 1 hectare = 2.47 acres.
Source: China Statistical Yearbook (various issues) and USDA, Interagency Commodity Estimates Committees, 2014b.

Figure 3
Geographic distribution of cotton area in China

- Yellow numbers indicate the percent each province contributed to the total national production. Provinces not numbered contributed less than 1% to the national total.
- Major areas combined account for 75% of the total national production.
- Major and minor areas combined account for 99% of the total national production.

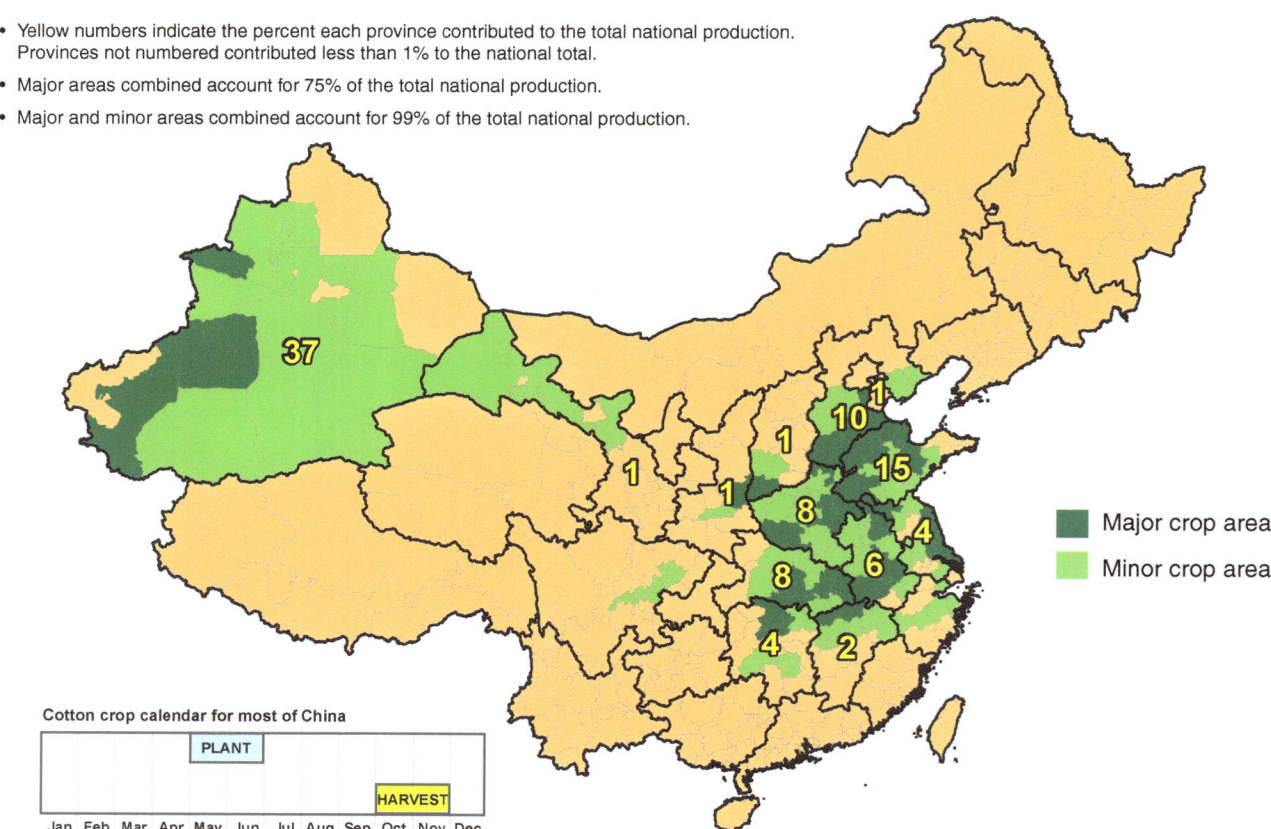

Note: Major and minor areas and provincial production percentages are derived from prefecture-level and provincial production data from 2008-2010. These data were obtained from provincial agricultural departments.
Source: Map used by permission of USDA, World Agricultural Outlook Board.

Cotton production is more labor-intensive than the production of grains and oilseeds in China, particularly given recent trends. One trend is that labor-saving technology has been adapted more quickly in the production of other commodities as China's population growth has slowed, its wages have risen, and labor per cultivated unit of land has fallen. Over the last decade, the labor intensity of cotton production has been declining 3 percent annually. The greater adoption of mechanization has resulted in annual declines ranging from 4 to 7 percent for other crops. Cotton harvesting technology has long been dominated by equipment designed for large-scale operations in the United States and the Soviet Union. Smaller scale equipment is under development in China and India, but has not been an option to date. Figure 4 shows trends in spending for mechanical harvesting and tillage by crop in China, with cotton at the lowest level of mechanization and slowest rate of growth. With China's wages rising at double-digit rates over the last decade, the labor-share of cotton production costs has risen from the 52 percent of the early 1990s to 68 percent nationally—and has approached 80 percent in provinces outside of Xinjiang. Measured as share of the value of crop output, the different labor share trends for cotton and other crops are quite clear: in 2000 and the years immediately afterward, cotton and other crops were similar in their labor shares, but since then labor cost shares have increased for cotton relative to other crops (fig 5).

Figure 4
Mechanization accelerates for crops other than cotton

Mechanization expenditures, share of crop value
Percent

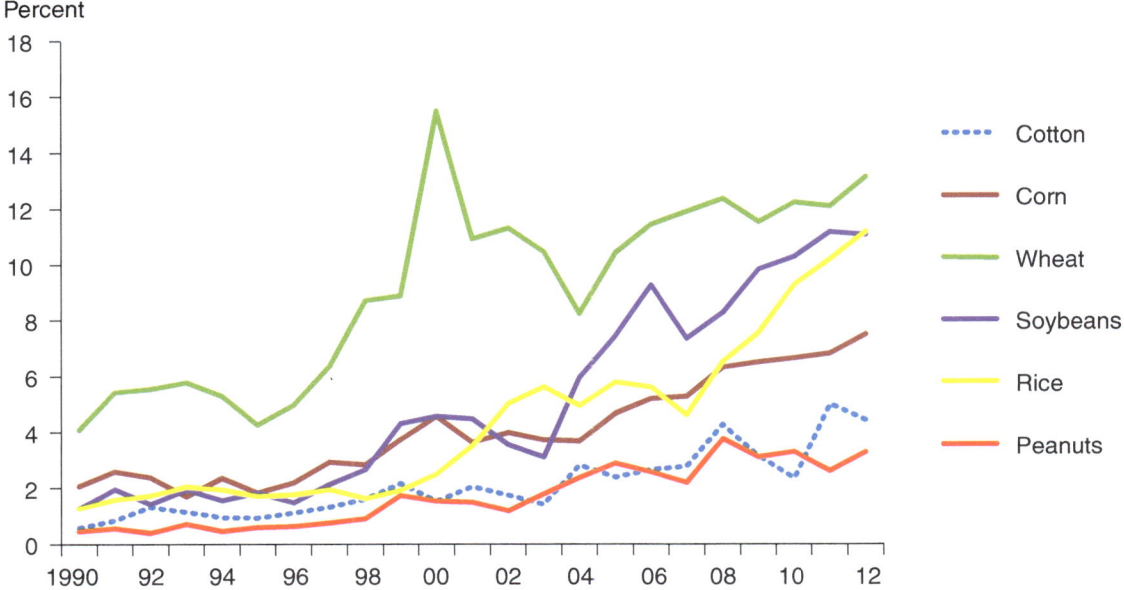

Source: USDA, Economic Research Service using data from from National Development and Reform Commission, *China agricultural production costs and returns compilation*, various issues.

Figure 5
Labor's share rising for China's cotton production

Labor costs, share of crop value
Percent

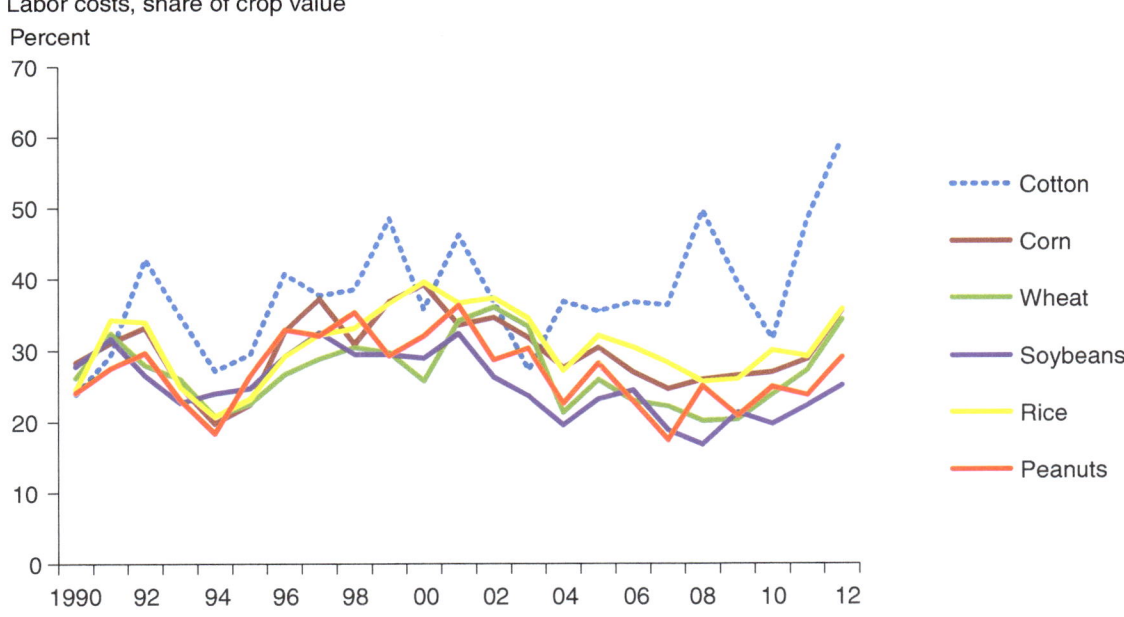

Source: USDA, Economic Research Service using data from from National Development and Reform Commission, *China agricultural production costs and returns compilation*, various issues.

China's Textile Sector

China's textile industry is the world's largest by a wide margin. China's households are a large market for clothing in their own right, but currently China's role as the major fabric and clothing supplier for the rest of the world is just as important in determining the amount of cotton fiber used by China's textile industry. Clothing imports in China are negligible, but China's exports are enormous—equivalent to almost 30 percent of the rest of the world's consumption. In 2010, more than half of the world's household consumption of textile products was produced in China, and about half of the output of China's textile industry is exported each year.[1] China's share of world trade in textiles rose every year between 1998 and 2013, rising from 13 to 37 percent over this period despite significant increases in wages and an appreciating currency during much of this time (table 1). The continued increases in China's share of the world's textile trade during 2010-13 are particularly significant, given the cumulative effects of wage increases and currency appreciation after 2005.

Textiles account for more than 10 percent of industrial employment in China, but only 5 percent of the value of industrial output. China's textiles and apparel trade surplus is as large as China's total merchandise trade surplus and is larger than the surplus of any other sector of the economy.[2] Textiles and apparel also have the highest share of domestically created value-added in their exports of any sector (OECD, 2013a). While China has successfully pursued technology transfer and upgrading in many industries (Studwell, 2013), the increasing sophistication of China's exports over the past 10 years is to a significant degree a function of the increasing sophistication of the imports it processes (Wang and Wei, 2008; Amiti and Fruend, 2010). This suggests that textiles have the potential to remain an important industry in China in future years: China's global role in the more capital-intensive portion of the industry (yarn and fabric) could remain strong even as the country faces increasingly intense competition in labor-intensive clothing production as China's wages rise.

Table 1
Overview of China's textile and apparel sector

	1997	2000	2005	2007	2012	2013
Employment (millions)	10.7	8.1	9.8	10.9	9.7	NA
Share of industrial output (%)	12.9	10.3	6.5	6.5	5.3	NA
Share of total exports (%)	25.0	20.9	15.1	14.1	12.4	12.9
Sector trade surplus/GDP (%)	3.4	3.2	4.3	4.4	2.8	2.8
Apparel share in sector exports (%)	69.7	69.1	64.4	67.3	62.6	62.5
Sector share of world trade (%)	13.7	14.7	24.1	29.3	36.0	37.1

NA = Data not available.

Source: Brandt, Rawski, and Sutton, 2008; China Statistical Yearbook, 2013; Alpermann, 2010; and World Trade Organization, 2014.

---

[1]The role of exports is minimized in most published summaries of China's textile industry. The widely reported 84-percent domestic market share for sales by China's textile industry (Sun, 2013) is inflated by including the 44 percent of those sales that are comprised of intra-industry consumption of intermediate inputs (National Bureau of Statistics, 2014a). The Food and Agriculture Organization and International Cotton Advisory Committee's *World Apparel Consumption Survey* (FAO/ICAC, 2013) indicates that China's textile exports and domestic end-use were about evenly matched in 2010. China's National Bureau of Statistics (NBS) survey data indicate that 2010-12 household spending on clothing equals 55-60 percent of total industry adjusted sales value and World Trade Organization export data also equal about 55-60 percent of these adjusted sales.

[2]Note that China's total trade surplus is the net of the large surpluses in textiles and electronics and the large deficits in petroleum, agriculture, and other raw materials.

China's Cotton Policy

China's agricultural policy is oriented toward maintaining food security, improving the well-being of China's farmers, and guiding the development and modernization of the agricultural sector. Government support for cotton through payments to producers has been smaller than that for grains (see box, "Pre-2014 Subsidies for Cotton Production"). Managing grain production and supplies has long been the central concern of China's agricultural policy, and food security has traditionally been perceived as synonymous with self-sufficiency in grains. In part this has been a strategic decision, but it is also a component of broader economic policy. Food is a higher share of consumer expenditures in China than clothing (36 percent versus 11 percent), and the management of inflationary expectations requires closer attention to the volatility of grain prices than to cotton prices.

Pre-2014 Subsidies for Cotton Production

The main direct subsidies for China's cotton farmers before 2014 were a small payment for planting superior cotton varieties and for discounted crop insurance. China's agricultural subsidies are largely directed toward grain producers and in 2012 equaled about 9 percent of the value of China's agricultural production (Gale, 2013). Cotton producers benefit indirectly from many of the subsidies ostensibly for grains, partly due to the diversity of many farmers' cropping patterns, which means cotton farmers often also produce grains, and partly due to the imprecise nature of some provinces' subsidy distribution. Where farm specialization is greater, a differential impact of grain subsidies can be observed, indicating that cotton production has sometimes not been supported by the grain subsidies (Meng, 2012). Cotton producers in eastern China also are typically unable to access China's $2 billion to $3 billion annual machinery subsidy as farm size and cultivation practices there impede mechanization of cotton harvesting. This puts cotton production at a relative disadvantage in these provinces as mechanized harvesting becomes increasingly common for grains. China's machinery subsidy regulations do have provisions that facilitate application to cotton harvesters, by raising the per-unit ceiling above the level fixed for grain harvesters. But only producers in the Xinjiang Region have sufficient scale to benefit from the program.

In addition to the superior seed variety subsidy, cotton producers in Xinjiang benefit from a subsidy for the transportation of cotton from Xinjiang to eastern China, where most of China's textile industry is located. Financing for traders and mills to purchase cotton from farmers is also subsidized through loans with preferential interest rates and conditions from the State-owned Agricultural Development Bank of China (ADBC).[1] Reportedly about half of China's harvest is purchased in most years with ADBC loans, and almost the entire crop in Xinjiang. ICAC (2013) estimates annual expenditure on the superior variety subsidy and Xinjiang transportation subsidy at about $150 million each, or a total of about 2 percent of the value of China's cotton crop. The value of the ADBC's preferential credit terms is likely of similar magnitude, based on the spread between published ADBC rates and commercial rates for rural loans (Gale and Collender, 2006). At times, further support has been granted by forgiving repayment of ADBC loans. While ADBC repayment rates have been reportedly high since 2009, Alpermann (2010) reports that in 2007 the Central Government cancelled 5.3 billion renminbi ($760 million) of ADBC debt for cotton companies in Xinjiang.

---

[1]ADBC is one of China's "policy" banks, and is distinct from the Agricultural Bank of China, which is more market-oriented.

China's grains policies also distinguish between the staple grains, rice and wheat, and feed grains such as corn. Policy for rice and wheat is explicitly described as a minimum procurement price policy, and a policy of complete or virtual self-sufficiency in these grains can be expected for the foreseeable future (Zhu, 2011; Gale, 2013). Policy for corn, while in many respects similar to that for wheat and rice, is distinguished from staple grains policy as being based on a system of ad hoc temporary buying and storage. During 2014, agricultural commodities receiving this treatment included rapeseed and sugar, and, for a period beginning in 2011, cotton was included in this category as well.

At the commodity level, agricultural policy is comprised of a set of interlocking measures regarding prices, management of intervention stocks and reserves, trade policy, and subsidies (fig 6). With cotton-specific subsidies relatively limited until 2014, price support has been the primary source of assistance to cotton production and cotton has consistently received higher levels of price support than other commodities since 2002 (OECD, 2013b).[3] China's trade policy for cotton can be best understood in most years as a component of price support measures, and intervention purchases of cotton during 2011-13 were nearly entirely aimed at maintaining high prices.

Figure 6
China's cotton policies

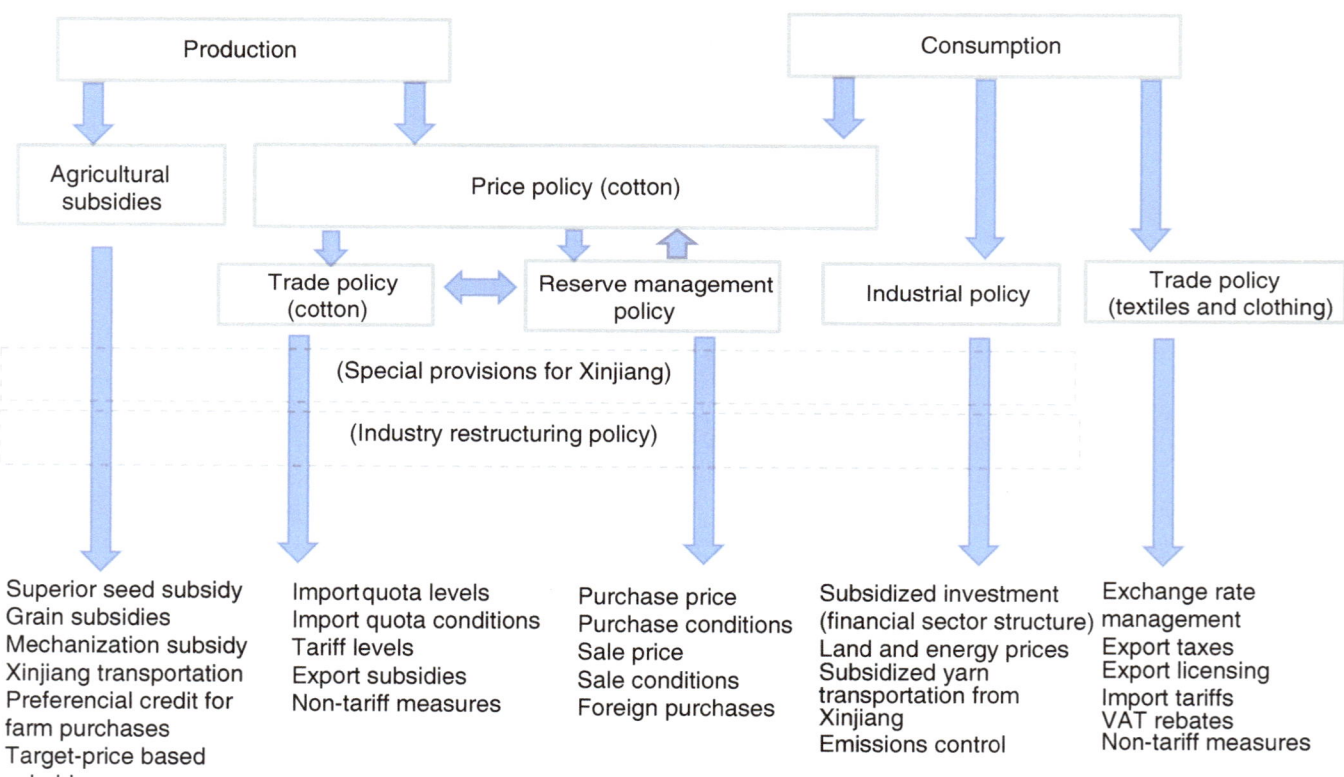

VAT = value-added tax.
Note: Xinjiang-Uygur Autonomous Region is China's largest cotton-growing province.
Source: USDA, Economic Research Service.

---

[3]Note that the measurement we describe as price support is virtually the same as OECD's "market price support." Both are similar to nominal rate of assistance (NRA) described by Anderson et al., 2008.

Price Support

Until the latter half of the 1990s, China's domestic prices were below equivalent international reference prices, indicating a price policy that was taxing rather than subsidizing farmers. Since the late 1990s, China has been providing significant support to its farmers by sustaining its domestic cotton prices above world levels (fig. 7). A "soft" version of this approach to supporting farmers developed in the years shortly after China's accession to the World Trade Organization (WTO) in December 2001, but in 2011 the policy became more formal and the support it provided increased. The price policy for cotton was "soft" because it did not include designated minimum prices publicly backed by a guarantee of public stock acquisition. In contrast, starting in 2004, grains and some other commodities increasingly received formal support as price floor guarantees (wheat and rice) or temporary buying and storage programs (corn, sugar, rapeseed, and soybeans) were introduced, and subsidies for area planted to grains and inputs for grain production were provided as well.

On occasion, cotton prices in China were supported by stock acquisition, and the Government maintained a cotton "guide" price between its 1999 cotton market liberalization and the 2011 introduction of a formal price support system for cotton (table 2). Direct subsidies for cotton were relatively limited (see box, "Pre-2014 Subsidies for Cotton Production," p. 7), and most support for cotton farmers had its source in a system where import tariffs, import quotas, and discretionary intervention purchases by the Government were applied in concert to keep the farm price about 50 percent above farm-equivalent world prices.[4]

Figure 7
China's cotton prices relative to border prices

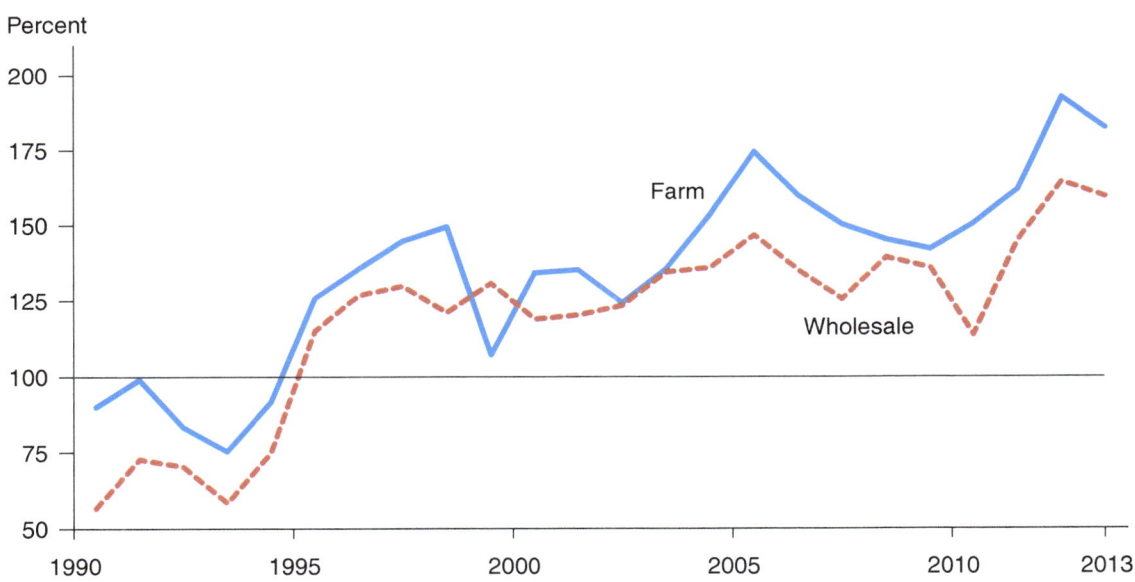

Source: USDA, Economic Research Service using data from National Development and Reform Commission, *China agricultural production costs and returns compilation*; Beijing Cotton Outlook; Zhu, 2001; Cotlook Ltd; Organization for Economic Cooperation and Development, 2013b; and International Monetary Fund, 2014a.

---

[4]Kwiecinski and Broussard (2013) report a survey of industry participants in China indicates a 28-percent marketing margin between the farm and wholesale level and a 4-percent transportation margin between ports and textile mills. Farm prices reported by China's National Development and Reform Commission were adjusted accordingly for comparison with border prices.

Table 2
Activity to support cotton policy in China typically conducted at prices close to world prices before 2011

	1999	2000	2001	2002	2003	2004	2005	2006	2007	2008	2009	2010	2011	2012	2013	2014
	U.S. dollars per metric ton (rounded)															
World price[1]	1,200	1,300	900	1,100	1,500	1,100	1,300	1,300	1,500	1,500	1,400	3,000	2,300	2,000	2,000	1,900
Guide price[2]	1,100	--	900	1,000	--	1,200	1,200	1,400	1,500	1,600	1,700	--	--	--	--	--
Reserve purchase	--	--	--	--	--	1,400	--	1,600	1,800	1,800	2,000	--	3,100	3,300	3,300	--
Reserve sale	1,400	1,400	1,100	--	--	--	--	--	1,600	--	--	2,900	--	3,100	3,000	--
Sliding-scale quota (SSQ) tariff price band																
Low tariff reference price[3]	--	--	--	--	--	--	1,200	1,300	1,500	1,600	1,700	1,700	1,700	2,200	2,200	2,500
Maximum price attracting peak tariff[4]	--	--	--	--	--	--	900	1,000	800	800	900	900	900	900	1,000	1,100
	Percent															
Farm price premium to world price	7	34	35	24	36	53	74	60	50	45	42	50	62	93	79	--
Spot price premium to world price	26	14	16	19	29	31	41	30	21	34	31	9	39	58	53	--
"Target" SSQ tariff[5]	--	--	--	--	--	--	5	14	12	8	7	16	4	3	8	10

[1]Cotlook A Index, average during months of policy price application.
[2]Average of guide prices, alert prices, and procurement prices reported in marketing year.
[3]Reference price (cost, insurance, and freight (cif)) for lowest tariff on cotton imported under sliding scale quota (calendar year).
[4]Level of cif price at which sliding scale tariff reaches maximum of 40 percent (calendar year).
[5]Tariff rate in calendar year if world price and exchange rate remain at previous year's average.

Source: USDA, Economic Research Service based on data from Cotlook Ltd; Cotton Outlook, various issues; Shi, 2000; and International Monetary Fund.

During 2011-13, China shifted to a formal price support system for cotton through the creation of a temporary reserve purchase program. The program offered farmers a minimum guaranteed price of 18,800 renminbi per ton (RMB/t), and then 19,400 RMB/t, backed by the Government's intention to purchase cotton during harvest when market prices fell below the announced threshold. These prices were the equivalent of $2,950/t to $3,200/t, during a period when the median monthly world price was $2,000/t, and no monthly average exceeded $2,600 (fig. 8). China's 2011-13 price policy was in certain respects the culmination of evolving trends, but in other respects, the policy represented a significant break from longstanding practices. It was the culmination of recent trends in the sense that China has in general been increasing its support for agriculture (Gale, 2013), and China had raised its cotton farm prices relative to world prices since the 1990s. It was a break from past practice in the explicitness of the price guarantee to farmers, the divergence in the level of price support compared with other crops, and in the increase in the premium above world prices it imposed on textile mills in China during 2011-13 (table 3).

The formal price support program for cotton was introduced in March 2011, when world cotton prices were realizing their largest upward shock in about 150 years. Had prices remained closer to these high levels, the amount of price support provided by the temporary reserve purchase program would have been far less than was realized and it is reasonable to conclude that much of the resulting increase in the price support level was unintentional. While above 2005-10 price levels, the 2011 cotton reserve purchase price was significantly below the peak levels reached by other cotton prices. Table 4 indicates prices in China and around the world around the time of the reserve purchase program's introduction reached levels about 20 percent to 100 percent above China's support price. Note also that the increase in cotton prices came after a sustained increase in grain prices over the preceding 5 years. While the rapidly rising cost of cotton production in China was also a factor behind choosing a support price above historical levels, some proportion of the initial

Figure 8
World cotton and grain prices and China cotton reserve buying price

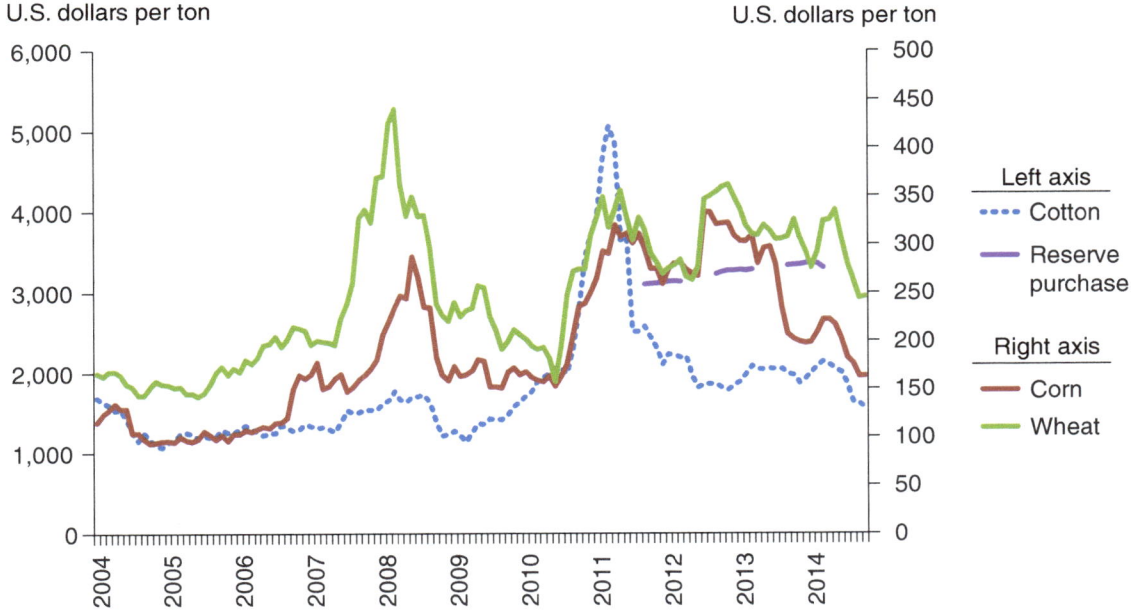

Source: Cotlook, Ltd; *Cotton Outlook*, various issues; International Monetary Fund, 2014a and 2014b.

Table 3

China's domestic cotton prices rise relative to world cotton price and other crop prices in China

	Wholesale cotton	Farm			
		Cotton	Wheat	Corn	Soybeans
		Ratio: domestic/world price (5-year average)			
1990-94	0.67	0.89	0.87	0.86	1.00
1995-99	1.25	1.33	1.36	1.43	1.37
2000-04	1.29	1.37	1.16	1.44	1.14
2005-09	1.36	1.54	1.08	1.37	1.22
2010-12	1.41	1.68	1.17	1.36	1.26

Source: USDA, Economic Research Service using data from Organization for Economic Cooperation and Development, 2013b, National Development and Reform Commission, China agricultural production costs and returns compilation, various issues; World Bank, 2007; Zhu, 2001; Beijing Cotton Outlook, 2014; and International Monetary Fund.

Table 4

World and China cotton prices relative to reserve purchase price, 2011 and 2013.

	Difference from reserve purchase price in:		
	Month of peak level[1]	November 2011	November 2013
	Percent		
China imports' average[2]	28	0	-18
U.S. exports' average[3]	40	6	-15
China farm[4]	36	0	NA
China spot price[5]	56	-3	-3
World price[5]	99	-10	-27
ZCE, nearby contract[6]	64	0	-3
ZCE, March 2012[7]	30	0	NA
ICE, nearby contract[5]	77	-16	-36
ICE, December 2011[7]	19	-16	NA
World price (forward)[7]	35	NA	NA

Note: Prices outside of China converted to China wholesale equivalent by adding transportation, tariffs, and marketing margins.
NA = data not available.
[1]Footnotes 2-7 indicate the month that each price's monthly average peaked. [2]May 2011. [3]June 2011. [4]November 2011. [5]March 2011. [6]February 2011. [7]April 2011.

Source: USDA, Economic Research Service using data from Cotton Outlook, various issues; Global Trade Information Service; National Bureau of Statistics; Cotlook Ltd; Zhengzhou Commodity Exchange (ZCE); InterContinental Exchange (ICE); and International Monetary Fund.

increase in price support that was realized after 2010 likely represented the expectation by Chinese policymakers of the permanence the 2010-11 world price increase.

Supporting farmers by using a combination of trade policy and intervention buying to raise domestic prices has the advantage of potentially limiting the direct expenditures needed by the Government to transfer resources to farmers. A disadvantage is that what is intended to be a producer price policy also affects consumers of the product, and the premium to world prices faced by China's textile mills rose from an average of 36 percent before 2011 to 64 percent during 2011-13. As a consequence, China's textile industry lost much of its international competitiveness in producing cotton yarn, and the industry's consumption of raw cotton fell 29 percent between the 2009 and 2013 marketing years. As high prices made spinning Chinese cotton uncompetitive, millions of tons of cotton flowed into the Chinese Government's intervention stockpiles, resulting in large expenditures for acquisition and storage.

China's policymakers have recently expressed interest in shifting much of their support for grains and agriculture to a target-price based system of subsidy payments akin to the U.S. system of target prices and deficiency payments that prevailed during 1985-96.[5] For cotton, Chinese policymakers indicated that the formal price support policy implemented during 2011-13 was found to be unsustainable due to falling consumption and rising stocks of raw cotton, and that starting with 2014 it would be significantly modified.[6] The focus of China's cotton policy shifted from its reliance on high prices to a greater reliance on Government subsidies paid directly to farmers, particularly for producers in Xinjiang. Cotton production in Xinjiang was designated as a pilot project for such a program, and a 2014 target price of 19,800 RMB/t, or 18,800 RMB/t ton ($3,010/t) at the farm level, was announced. This policy is consistent with past practice in extending preferential treatment to producers in Xinjiang, but marked the beginning of a significant shift from price support to income support for cotton.

During 2014, Chinese policymakers slowly reduced the price of cotton sold from China's intervention stockpiles. Due to the high degree of price uncertainty created by the size of China's stocks, a gradual approach to reducing prices and stocks may be the most appropriate way to manage the period of transition to China's new cotton policy mix.[7] These new policies include a return to the earlier "soft" price support policy and a lower level of price support.

---

[5]For more information, see "Drafting Team Member Cites Highlights of Central Document No. 1 on Food Security, Food Safety," *Renmin Ribao Online*, January 20, 2014.

[6]See USDA/FAS, 2014b for a summary.

[7]At China's State Reserve's annual Work Conference in February 2014, a senior official with the National Development and Reform Commission (NDRC) noted that purchasing by State reserves will remain an option given that there remains a "core objective … to protect farmers' interests in the new market environment." (*Beijing Zhongguo Jingji Daobao* Online, June 25, 2014, translation by Open Source Center). At the 2014 China Cotton Industry Development Summit Forum in Xiamen, Fuijan Province in May 2014, NDRC officials indicated that the Government intends to phase out its role in the market, but that it would be a "transitional process" (*Cotton Outlook*, Vol. 92, No. 20, May, 16, 2014).

Government Stockpile Management

China's cotton intervention stocks are managed as part of its cotton reserve.[8] Reserve levels during China's post-WTO-accession period have typically been near 15 percent of domestic consumption and accounted for about one-third of China's total cotton ending stocks. Ending stock levels relative to consumption in China are typically above the global average, perhaps reflecting the unusually large role of these Government-controlled stocks. Carter et al. (2012) noted that stocks in China's grain reserve were retained for longer periods and at higher levels than is consistent with just controlling price volatility. This may be an inherent result of Government buffer stock schemes—which often err on the side of supporting prices—or a function of the incentives for the State-owned enterprises (SOEs) responsible for managing stocks to maximize their revenue.[9] The longrun median stocks-to-use ratio in China is 53 percent, versus a comparable average level elsewhere in the world of 28 percent (fig. 9).[10]

Price support operations are implemented through domestic purchases by the reserve management authority—the China National Cotton Reserve Corporation (CNCRC)—but before 2011, the

Figure 9

China's stocks/use ratio (SU) and world and China cotton prices, 1970-2013

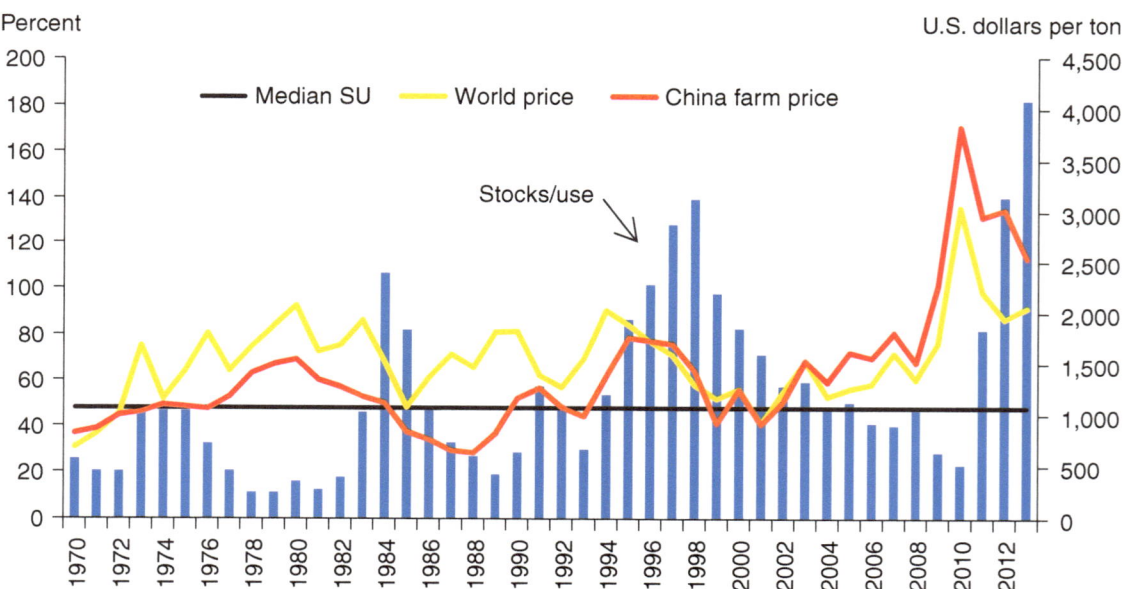

Source: USDA, Economic Research Service calculations based on data from USDA, Foreign Agricultural Service (2014b); World Bank (2007); National Development and Reform Commission; Colby, Crook, and Webb (1992); Cotlook Ltd.; and International Monetary Fund (2014a).

---

[8]China's Government maintains reserves of a wide variety of commodities including grain, vegetable oil, sugar, pork, petroleum and a wide variety of metals. A key function of China's reserve system is the management of price volatility.

[9]Policy implementation in China is often decentralized, creating opportunities for the self-interest of entities like reserve management firms to produce outcomes sometimes at variance from the objectives of central authorities. Alpermann (2010) recounts how in CNCRC's early years its speculative activities on its own account resulted in unplanned additions to the national reserve (pages 174-7).

[10]Calculated over 1990-2010.

benefits to farmers of these purchases were indirect and sometimes limited. Chinese farmers market their cotton as unginned seed cotton, but the reserve purchases only ginned bales of cotton fiber. The efficiency of China's agricultural markets mean that higher lint prices could be transmitted to farmers, but the largest reserve purchases during 2005-10 were initiated after farmers had already sold much of their cotton (Du, 2011). The reserve purchases of 2008-09 had an additional objective, altering the organization of China's cotton marketing and processing sector, and this also limited the program's impact on farmers. Beginning in 2008, with the goal of modernizing the ginning sector, reserve purchases were restricted to cotton baled to international standards (227-kilogram bales) and machine tested (classed using high-volume instrumentation, or HVI, rather than manual classification). Traditionally, most of China's cotton outside of Xinjiang was pressed into 85-kg bales, and consequently, prices were lower during the 2008/09 marketing year in regions where firms used the older equipment to a greater extent.

Sales from the reserve have been managed in varied ways as priorities have changed. In 2009 and 2010, reserve sales were undertaken to limit price increases, but in 2012 and 2013, the management of reserve sales was integrated with efforts to support the price. Reserve stocks were offered for sale, but with a price floor only 5 to 10 percent below the price of the reserve purchases (while the border price was 60 percent below the reserve purchase price). With a known price floor, the auctions for reserve cotton were more akin to a public component of an ongoing series of negotiations between the Government and the textile industry. For example, in April 2014, the reserve sales price target was revised down to 15 percent below the reserve purchase price as the government began shifting to a more flexible price support policy. The Government's limitation of cotton imports, which increases the market value of cotton in the reserve and allows the Government to link the distribution of import quota to purchases at the reserve auctions, is an integral component of the management of reserve sale prices. During 2012 and 2013, reserve sales totaled more than 6.5 million tons, more than 40 percent of CNCRC's 2011-13 purchases, but not enough to prevent the reserve from rising to an unprecedented level.

China's use of intervention buying to support cotton prices during 2011-13 was to some extent a break from its past practice, but such intervention was not completely absent before then. Between 2005 and 2010, intervention goals of raising and lowering prices were largely balanced, and intervention served to limit the volatility of China's cotton prices (table 5). However, intervention activity was also channeled to support China's industrial organization goals for the ginning industry. The break from the past during 2011-13 was that China's cotton stockpile management became primarily a price support mechanism, with stocks consequently growing to unprecedented size, and becoming a potential source of global price instability rather than an instrument of price stability. In 2014, the Government began reducing sales prices for its intervention stocks, signaling its intent to reduce price support levels.

Table 5

China's domestic cotton intervention purchases and sales, 2004-13

| | Purchases | Sales | Net purchases level | Net purchases as ratio to: | |
				China production	World consumption
	-------------Thousand tons------------			------------Percent------------	
2004	140	0	140	2	1
2005	10	0	10	0	0
2006	303	150	153	2	1
2007	0	0	0	0	0
2008	2,800	1,200	1,600	20	7
2009	0	1,400	-1,400	-20	-5
2010	0	1,000	-1,000	-15	-4
2011	3,130	0	3,130	42	14
2012	6,506	4,210	2,297	30	10
2013	6,307	2,316	3,992	56	17

Source: USDA, Economic Research Service using data from: International Cotton Advisory Committee *Review of the World Cotton Situation*, various issues; *Cotton Outlook*, various issues; USDA, Foreign Agricultural Service, 2014; and USDA, Interagency Commodity Estimates Committees, 2014a.

Trade Policy

Trade policy facilitates reserve management policy, but ultimately is also a supporting leg of China's goals for price support. Imports account for virtually all of China's cotton trade activity, and since its WTO accession, China's trade policy has been largely focused on managing these import flows to balance the competing interests of the textile industry and farmers. Import volume is largely a function of the amount of quota distributed by the Government and the conditions attached to the quotas. Import tariffs range from 0 to 40 percent, depending on the category of the imports and the year the cotton is imported, but most imports enter under the "sliding scale" quota (SSQ) and are charged a tariff of about 13 percent (27 percent with value-added tariff (VAT)—(see box, "China's Import Tariff Administration"). Policies determining the SSQ tariff level were crucial to determining the level of prices in China during 2005-10, with wholesale, or spot, prices varying from the duty-paid border price by less than 3 percent on average.[11]

The size, timing, and conditionality of quotas are the primary instruments determining China's cotton imports in most years, but in recent years two additional factors have been important. Both 2012 and 2013 were unusual in that a significant share of China's imports were those undertaken by State-owned enterprises for policy purposes, such as adding to the national reserve (fig. 10). "Policy" imports like these can be independent of the quotas issued to private and State-owned enterprises for commercial purposes, but the process is not transparent either at the initiation of such imports or in the disposition of the imported cotton. Also, in 2012 and 2013, out-of-quota cotton

Figure 10
China's imports by adminstrative category compared with excess demand[1]

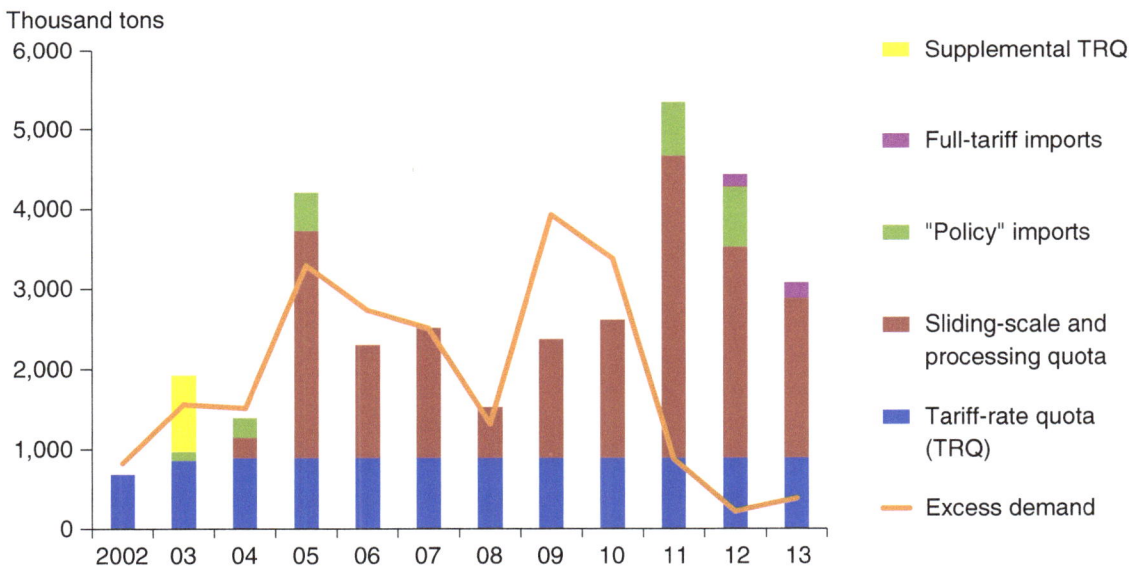

[1]Excess demand = consumption - production.
Source: USDA, Foreign Agricultural Service (FAS), 2014a; and USDA, Economic Research Service calculations using data from USDA/FAS, 2014b.

---

[11]The standard grade in China's cotton market has a 28-millimeter (mm) staple (fiber length). The wholesale price used in this report is the CC3128B reported by Beijing Cotton Outlook and the China National Cotton Exchange.

China's Cotton Import Tariff Administration

China's WTO accession agreement specified an 894,000-ton tariff-rate quota (TRQ) each year with a tariff of 1 percent, and the binding of non-TRQ cotton import tariffs at 40 percent, with discretion to manage its tariffs within this range.

Since 2003, China has unilaterally supplemented its TRQ with additional quota that has accounted for most of China's cotton trade. The supplemental quota issued through April 2005 was an extension of the TRQ, with a 1-percent tariff. Since then, the supplemental imports have been broken into those under a sliding-scale quota (SSQ) system and quota dedicated to processing for re-export. Processing cotton for re-export as textiles entitles the firm to duty drawback, so imports under processing quota are effectively charged a zero tariff. The SSQ tariff is determined through an annually reviewed formula that progressively raises tariffs from 3 to 5 percent up as far as the 40-percent bound rate when world prices fall. China's system of indirect taxation also boosts the level of border protection since farmers are exempt from the 13-percent value-added tax (VAT) that is applied to imported cotton. Furthermore, the VAT is assessed on the total value of the imported cotton and the trade duty, shifting the effective tariff on out-of-quota cotton from 40 percent up to 58 percent.

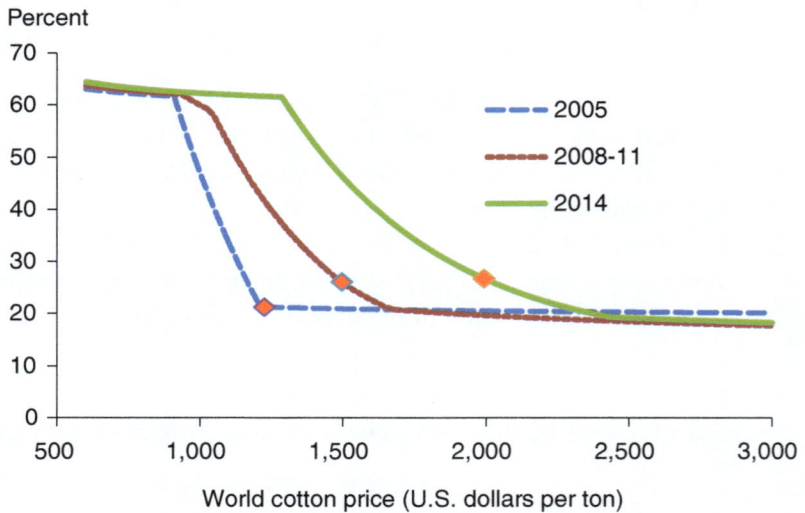

Variation in level of tariff protection under China's Sliding-Scale Quota (SSQ), 2005-14

Percent

World cotton price (U.S. dollars per ton)

Note: Diamonds indicate average price in previous year.
Average renminbi/U.S. dollar exchange rate of previous year used in calculations, and total tariff protection includes effect of 13-percent value-added tax.
Source: USDA, Economic Research Service using data from *Cotton Outlook*, various issues; and International Monetary Fund.

Because the majority of China's cotton imports enter under either the SSQ or processing quota programs, Chinese policymakers have a degree of flexibility in determining the average tariffs that apply to imported cotton. The tariff on SSQ imports is above 1 percent, so the transition in mid-2005 from unconditionally expanding the TRQ to the distribution of SSQ represented an increase in tariff protection for China's cotton farmers, with the trade-weighted 2005-2010 average tariff equal to 13 percent. By some measures, protection has risen during the lifetime of the SSQ program, since a border price of $1,350/t would have been taxed in 2005, 2008-11, and 2014 at 19 percent, 30 percent, and then 53 percent, respectively. But since nominal border prices for cotton in USD terms have trended upwards during this time the realized tariff level has remained relatively constant.

The 2014 SSQ tariff regulations give some clues regarding policymakers' future goals. A tariff level of 10 percent would apply if both the world price and the exchange rate in 2014 remained at year-earlier averages, and this is 1 percent above the average tariff that would have been projected using a similar methodology each year during 2006-13 (table 2). But the "Low tariff reference price" of about $2,500/ton is higher than any earlier such reference price and also includes the largest premium compared with the previous year's world price. Therefore, the SSQ tariff policy in 2014 is slightly more distortionary than it was before 2011.

imports occurred for the first time as China's policies boosted domestic market prices far enough above world prices to warrant imports with payment of the full tariff of 40 percent. These developments are indicative of the disruption and uncertainties engendered by China's cotton policies in recent years.

China uses adjustments in the SSQ tariff and aspects of its quota disbursement (size, timing, and conditions) to attempt to maintain domestic cotton prices within broad bands. Quota management is also used to meet other policy objectives, like support cotton production in Xinjiang, and is perhaps the policy variable that receives the most attention from market participants. How the tariffs applied to SSQ cotton are determined during a given year is a transparent process, but not so the determination of the annual volume of SSQ quota or the time of year it is released. The extent of disclosure about the level and timing of the quota release varies from year to year, depending on market conditions. Large volumes of quota have been very publicly released early in the calendar year during periods of high prices and rapidly growing textile production (in early 2004, for example). Quotas have been small, conditional on textile exports or sourcing from Xinjiang, and distributed discretely when prices are lower (as in early 2009).

In addition to supporting price policy, this discretionary approach to quota management affects the distribution of the rents produced by the trade restrictions.[12] Limiting the amount of unused quota at any time, and the creation of information asymmetry between a set of potential importers and the rest of the world, allows firms with privileged access to information to appropriate these rents rather than having them appropriated by foreign cotton exporters or the general population of domestic textile firms.[13] This is an aspect of China's industrial policy that favors selected larger firms in order to build technically advanced and globally competitive firms with strong vertical linkages throughout the supply chain (Alpermann, 2010).

Other conditions governing imports into China include the registration of the exporting firm with China's General Administration of Quality Supervision, Inspection and Quarantine (AQSIQ) and a set of phytosanitary and fiber quality inspection conditions. A 2011 study by USITC noted that China's customs clearance procedures for merchandise imports can be time-consuming, opaque, and ultimately expensive since in some cases traders come to rely on well-connected firms specializing in facilitating customs clearance (USITC, 2011). This is indicative of the existence of additional policy levers that could be utilized to limit imports that current, published regulations would suggest would otherwise be permitted. China permitted importation of cotton outside of its quotas in 2012 and 2013, but the experience of corn imports in recent years facing increasingly stringent phytosanitary requirements is an example of the application of new nontariff measures (NTM) that cannot be ruled out in the future for cotton. Quark (2014) details how China's cotton quality standards are evolving, suggesting that China's 2003 effort to introduce new quality requirements for cotton imports could be resurrected.

---

[12]An import license is a valuable commodity when quantitative restrictions constrain imports. The additional profits that accrue to the agents who receive benefits like an import license are described as rents (Krueger, 1974).

[13]de Gorter and Hranaiova (2004) summarize the economics of these and other aspects of import quota administration.

The Transition to Subsidy-based Support Begins in Xinjiang

Most of China's cotton policies include special provisions for the Xinjiang Region. Xinjiang is a relatively undeveloped province and agriculture accounts for about 18 percent of its gross domestic product (GDP)—twice the sector's share elsewhere in China—and cotton accounts for about 50 percent of Xinjiang's farm output versus 1 percent to 3 percent in the rest of China. Xinjiang is a strategic concern of the Central Government because it is the province furthest from China's capital and its main population centers and because of the unusually large share of its population that is ethnically, linguistically, and religiously distinct from the majority of China's population.

Xinjiang's great distance from the regional concentrations of China's textile industry as well as the occurrence of violent disruptions there[14] hamper the region's effectiveness as a source of China's cotton fiber. Furthermore, Xinjiang is one of driest areas in the world, and large increases in the province's population, industrial output, and agriculture have resulted in an the acceleration of desertification and soil salinization, and in rising salinity and severely diminished downstream flow for the Tarim River (Feike et al., 2015). On the other hand, Xinjiang offers an ideal environment for irrigated agriculture (Orenstein et al., 2011). Per-hectare yields there far surpass those elsewhere in China and climate change is bolstering irrigation supplies at the headwaters of the rivers (Piao et al., 2010), and the opportunities for the region to shift to mechanical harvesting in response to rising wages are demonstrably far greater than elsewhere in China. The Xinjiang Production and Construction Corps (XPCC), a SOE that accounts for nearly half of the province's production, was harvesting much of its cotton mechanically by 2013.[15] Due to climate, larger scale production, and technical sophistication, the region's cotton has long been considered of higher quality than that of other provinces. The combination of resource endowments and central Government priorities suggest that Xinjiang will account for an increasing share of China's cotton output as China's cotton policies and industry evolve.

The distinction between cotton policy in Xinjiang and the rest of China became particularly acute when cotton procurement was officially privatized and price determination within China largely freed from state controls in 1999. A fixed-price system remained in Xinjiang for an additional year after the termination of such prices in the rest of China, and the effective privatization of much of China's cotton procurement companies had less impact in Xinjiang.[16] While in principle, the goal of China's domestic cotton policy is to use reserve purchases to boost low prices for all farmers, reserve purchases in practice have been skewed toward supporting Xinjiang, and trade policy also has preferentially benefited cotton from Xinjiang. In 2006, 700,000 tons of import quota were set aside as awards to textile mills that purchased cotton from Xinjiang enterprises. In 2014, access to State reserve stocks of imported cotton was linked in a 1:3 ratio to purchases of Xinjiang cotton from the State reserve. This was during a period when textile mills were allotted 1 ton of sliding-scale quota for every 4 tons of non-Xinjiang cotton they purchased from the reserve.

---

[14]In 2009 China cut Xinjiang's internet access to the rest of the world for 10 months following riots in which about 200 people reportedly died (Hogg, 2010).

[15]The XPCC has played a leading role in the development of Xinjiang's cotton industry, and in other parts of the province's economy. The XPCC is administratively separate and equivalent to the provincial government.

[16]Partly, this reflected specific policy decisions, but also reflected the unusually large share for State-owned farms in the province's cotton output.

In 2014, a new crucial distinction emerged between policies for Xinjiang and the rest of China with the introduction of target-price-based subsidies heavily weighted in favor of producers in Xinjiang. Under this target-price policy, Xinjiang producers will sell seed cotton to certified ginners at market prices. Depending on the difference between a target price of 19,800 RMB/t[17] and the market price during the first 3 months of the marketing year, cotton farmers will either receive no subsidy (if the market price equals or exceeds the target price) or a payment equal to the difference between the prices. At the time the 2014 target price was announced, it was about 27 percent higher than cotton imported with SSQ (adjusted for the Xinjiang transportation subsidy). The substantially larger average farm size in Xinjiang—particularly in the XPCC—will help mitigate the inefficiencies and difficulties inherent in the distribution of direct payments to China's myriad small farmers (Huang et al., 2013).

Farmers in other provinces will receive a fixed subsidy of 2,000 RMB/t for receipts for cotton delivered to qualified purchasing and processing enterprises. Funds for the subsidy payments will be made available to the provincial governments within a month of the National Bureau of Statistics' verification of provincial production levels. At the time this policy was announced, 2,000 RMB/t was about 40 percent of the expected target-price based subsidy for Xinjiang farmers. A plan to offer subsidies in future seasons in these provinces was also announced, with subsidies up to 60 percent of the Xinjiang subsidy, but capped at 2,000 RMB/t.

The Xinjiang subsidies also serve to support mechanization. Mechanical picking introduces larger amounts of plant material into the harvested cotton, and during 2014, farm prices for mechanically harvested cotton were about 10 percent lower than those for hand-picked. Under the pilot program, subsidies for mechanically harvested cotton in 2014 are higher, since the target price is the same for both. In future years—as the varieties planted and other aspects of cotton production, ginning, and cotton spinning shift to meet the requirements of mechanical harvesting—some of this price differential could disappear, but in the meantime, the program helps subsidize modernization as well as the level of production by effectively eliminating this price differential for the producer.[18]

---

[17]18,800 RMB/t ($3,010/t) at the farm level, after accounting for ginning costs.

[18]The more extensive cleaning gins undertake with mechanically harvested cotton helps account for the greater prevalence of short fibers and neps (tangled fibers) compared with cotton harvested by hand, and the price discount. The likely rapid increase in the mechanically harvested share of China's cotton production has implications for the evolution of China's goals in international negotiations over cotton quality standards. This aspect of China's cotton policy is beyond the scope of this report, but is detailed in Quark, 2014.

Outlook for China's Cotton Policy

China's cotton policies will evolve based on continued movement toward a market-driven economy, balancing the interests of Chinese cotton farmers against those of textile manufacturers, disposal of the country's large cotton stocks, and compliance with World Trade Organization commitments.

The broadest sign of relevant economic policy objectives that will guide future cotton policy is found in the November 2013 Communique of the 3rd Plenum Session of the Central Committee, which highlighted the new leadership's intention to stress the "decisive" role of the market in the allocation of resources. Consistent with this, the State Council in January 2014 confirmed that support in the form of direct payments would be implemented in Xinjiang in 2014, with the aim of eventually decoupling the cotton price from Government support, and returning the price generating power to the market. Subsequently, a series of articles in China's official press confirmed a general policy goal for agriculture of,

> "...turning price support into income support, as well as reduce government intervention in the market, so that prices can fully reflect the changes in supply and demand...."
> (*Beijing Zhongguo Jingji Baobao*, June 25, 2014, translation by Open Source Center)

The structure of the 2014 cotton subsidy program also gives indications of Chinese policymakers' future intentions for cotton policy. Indicative of the new resolve to reduce market distortions is the application of a target price below the 2012 and 2013 support prices. Another indication is the even lower support for cotton production outside of Xinjiang: the variable, target-price-based subsidy is exclusive to Xinjiang and the national minimum price program was not renewed during a period of declining reserve sales prices. The 2014 program for producers outside of Xinjiang included a substantially less generous fixed 2,000 RMB/t subsidy.

Another indicative policy decision set the 2014 regulations for the level of the SSQ tariff. A clue to intentions in the level of price support is found in the similarity between the 2014 SSQ "target tariff" and the pre-2011 level of this tariff. Defining the "target tariff" as the tariff that would apply to SSQ imports if the world price of cotton and China's exchange rate in 2014 matched their year-earlier levels, the 2014 target tariff of 10 percent equates to a 27-percent level of border protection once VAT and other charges are included. This is very close to the 25-percent historic average of the VAT-adjusted target tariff over the 8 full years of the SSQ program, During 2005-10, the premium of China's wholesale domestic cotton price relative to the world price varied little from equivalence with the prevailing VAT-adjusted SSQ tariff.

These policy signals suggest that the level of price support for cotton will fall in the short run and, in the long run, may return to close to its historic mean. A complete removal of the wedge between world and domestic prices is not expected since support for prices is a longstanding component of China's cotton policy and maintaining a minimum price limits the direct budgetary expenditures for the newly introduced subsidies (table 6).[19] Thus, the most likely scenario for China's future price support is a return to its 2005-10 average level. This would be a reduction of the premium to the world price received by farmers from the 2011-13 average of 74 percent to 50 percent. At the wholesale level, it would be a reduction from 50 to 60 percent to 25 to 30 percent. This is consis-

---

[19]A target-price-based subsidy program results in payments to farmers equaling the difference between the target price and the prevailing market price. By limiting imports, raising the tariff on imports, or by increasing reserve purchases, the Government can raise the market price and reduce the magnitude of the difference between the target price and the market price.

tent with USDA's 2014 baseline, which has China's share of world cotton consumption partly rebounding to 37 percent, compared with 33 percent during 2012-14, as China's price distortion declines.[20]

Table 6

Goals and options for China's policymakers: Price policy for cotton

Goal	Instrument	Negative impacts	Positive impacts
Support cotton farmers with less price distortion	Target-price based direct subsidy	Adds budgetary exposure to support policy	Supplements incomes of farmers; helps reduce damaging indirect tax on textile industry
	Price support (PS) at 2005-10 level	Textile industry may be more susceptible to cost pressure than in 2005-10	Compared with no PS, reduces budgetary exposure of direct subsidy; compared with 2011-13 PS, reduces price distortion
	Align reserve purchase price during harvest more closely to world price	Potentially large welfare losses for producers excluded from direct subsidy program	Continuation of seasonal reserve buying allows stock rotation, limits intraseasonal price volatility

Source: USDA, Economic Research Service.

---

[20]Note that China's share of world consumption is forecast to remain well below its 2009 level of 42 percent.

Cotton Reserve Management: Outlook and Impact

China's future treatment of its 2011-13 reserve stock gains is less clear than its plans for cotton subsidies, but the high cost of maintaining these stocks, along with historical precedent, suggests stocks will fall significantly. Both trade policy and reserve sales policies must shift from 2011-13 patterns for this to occur, and large Government expenditures will be necessary to either maintain or reduce stocks. The greater the pace and extent of China's reduction in its reserves, the greater the negative price impact on the rest of the world during the period of stock reduction.

Due to the high prices paid for the cotton in the reserve as of 2014, and the much lower expected prices during the years that reserve sales would occur (USDA/OCE, 2015), feasible reserve sale prices imply substantial monetary losses. More than $6 billion would be lost selling 8 million tons of cotton at 2013 prices.[21] If world prices fall 10 percent, these losses rise to more than $8 billion. On the other hand, savings accrue from smaller storage expenditures when the reserve is smaller. In addition to the $2 billion needed to cover the annual cost of warehousing a 12-million-ton reserve, storage expenditures include financing costs by the Agricultural Development Bank of China (ADBC) and the loss in value due to deterioration. The lower costs associated with an 8-million-ton reduction in the size of the reserve could result in savings totaling $5 billion to $8 billion compared with retaining a 12-million-ton reserve through 2019. Retaining the cotton would only postpone losses, while continuing to incur the expenses.

China's disposal of a large cotton stockpile in the early 2000s may provide some guidance about how Chinese authorities might dispose of their current stockpile. By 1999, China had accumulated large cotton stocks (140 percent of use), which they reduced to 48-percent stocks-to-use by 2004. World and Chinese cotton prices during this period were substantially lower than during 1996-98 when the stocks were acquired. Central Government funds were used to offset the differences in price, which were as high as 44 percent (table 7). In total, 3.7 million tons of cotton were auctioned over 5 years—equaling as much as 7 percent of annual world consumption at the auctions' peak. Although the release was spread over 5 years, there was downward pressure on China's imports, domestic cotton prices, and world cotton prices. A drawdown of U.S. stocks in the 1960s also provides precedent. It took about 6 years to bring the 1965 stocks-to-use ratio of 135 percent back down to the longrun U.S. median ratio of 32 percent.[22]

For China to manage its costs of reducing cotton stocks will require a coordinated set of trade and intervention stock management policies (table 8), including:

1) setting the prices and conditions for reserve purchases during harvest

2) managing imports: reducing the level of SSQ and processing quota and determining whether to again increase the level of foreign cotton in the reserve through policy imports

---

[21]USDA's 2014 baseline projects average China cotton consumption during 2014-2023 of 10.2 million tons. China's longrun median stocks-use ratio is 53 percent, suggesting equilibrium stocks of 5.4 million tons, which would be 8 million tons below 2013 ending stocks.

[22]A 35-percent ratio was reached in 5 years, and 28 percent in 6 years. In 1985, the United States had stocks at 112 percent of use, but this was largely a function of a 68-percent decline in exports that was immediately reversed the following year.

Table 7

China's cotton sales from Government stocks (national reserve), 1999-2003

| Marketing year | Reserve sales | | | Domestic cotton price | |
| | | Sales ratio to: | | | |
	Sales level	World consumption	China production	Price level	Discount from 1996-98
	Tons	Percent		US $/ton	Percent
1999	656	3	17	1,296	-30
2000	1,413	7	32	1,364	-26
2001	352	2	7	1,028	-44
2002	1,078	5	20	1,441	-22
2003	150	1	3	1,943	6

Source: USDA, Economic Research Service using data from USDA, Foreign Agricultural Service, 2014; Beijing Cotton Outlook; International Cotton Advisory Committee *Review of the World Cotton Situation*, various issues; *Cotton Outlook*, various issues; Zhu, 2001; and USDA, International Commodity Estimates Committee, 2014a.

Table 8

Goals and options for China's policymakers: Reserve management for cotton

Goal	Instruments	Negative impacts	Positive impacts
National cotton reserve efficiency (lower stocks)	Align reserve sales price more closely to world price	Losses realized on sales of discounted cotton; world price declines likely with greater sales from reserve	Facilitates larger volume of sales from reserve and helps raise the competitiveness of domestic cotton yarn industry
	Limit non-TRQ imports	World price declines likely with cuts in imports;	Creates domestic market for sales from reserve; enables price support for cotton farmers
	Higher policy share of imports; access to foreign cotton channeled through reserve authorities	Efficiency of textile industry reduced through reduced direct contact with foreign exporters	Links industry's need for foreign cotton with policy goal of transferring domestic reserve cotton into market
	Permit or facilitate exports	May require subsidies and/or lower price support	Reduce net imports while retaining textile industry's direct access to imported cotton

Source: USDA, Economic Research Service.

3) funding financial losses by accepting prices for sales from the reserves below the 2011-13 average purchase price of $3,250/t

4) determining annual goals for the volume of sales from the reserve

Domestic cotton purchasing by the reserve will likely continue in order to reduce the average age and degree of deterioration of the reserve cotton, and also to manage intraseasonal price volatility. Harvest-time purchases for the reserve during a period of long-term stock drawdown will then drive a higher level of reserve sales after the harvest. Assuming the Chinese Government applies a harvest purchase price consistent with its postharvest sales price, these additional transactions will not add substantial net costs to stocks management. Alternatively, the process could be a channel for providing support to Chinese cotton farmers through a higher purchase price, while maintaining the textile industry's access to relatively competitively priced cotton.

Trade policy will likely adjust to restrict net imports proportional to the extent that smaller stocks are a goal, and this will be one of the channels through which the rest of the world will be affected by China's policy changes (see "Estimated Price Impact of China's Cotton Stock Changes" section below). Additional trade policy issues flow from the fact that China's textile industry has traditionally required a substantial amount of foreign cotton for either blending or direct use to meet quality standards, because most of China's cotton is handpicked and is therefore more prone to contamination from other fibers than is cotton from many exporting countries.[23] USDA estimates indicated that the reserve contained little imported cotton at the end of 2013/14, so successfully diverting textile mill purchasing from imports to the national reserve may require that China raise the policy share of non-TRQ imports and expanding the bundling of sales of domestic and foreign cotton from the reserve. It may even be necessary to seek export markets for China's cotton, allowing a higher level of imports to be associated with a given level of reserve reduction. Exports currently are only permitted by SOEs, and given the current differentials between world and Chinese prices they do not seem feasible. Note that China's WTO accession agreement does not include any permissible level of cotton export subsidies.[24] If an aggressive program of reserve sales and a lower than average price support level brings China's prices significantly closer to world prices, two-way trade of cotton differentiated by quality and season may be feasible for China.

The above policies will have to be coordinated with each other and with the management of sales from the reserves. For example: the Chinese Government will find it difficult to find buyers for reserve cotton if it fixes the reserve sales price too high, and whether a reserve sale price is too high will be determined by the world price of cotton and the competitiveness of China's cotton yarn producers. The interaction between China's stock changes, China's imports, and world prices will constrain Chinese policymakers' choices, because an effort to minimize losses on reserve cotton sales by fixing a high reserve price and restricting the availability of imports will reduce the world price. In turn, the combination of a low world price and high domestic price would damage the competitiveness of China's cotton yarn producers, and reduce their ability to purchase reserve cotton. Thus, an effort to minimize current expenditures on stock disposal might conflict with goals to reduce long-term stock levels and storage expenses.

The pace of stock reduction will be factor in determining the magnitude of financial losses on reserve sales. With the world price at 2013 levels, reserve sale prices would have to be discounted nearly 25 percent from the average 2011-13 reserve purchase price if China's price falls to its historical level of relative to global prices. Since the 2015 USDA baseline projects 2014-19 prices to be 20 percent below 2013 levels, reserve sales prices would likely be 45 percent below the purchase price during those years. USDA's baseline projects China's stocks-use ratio at 73 percent in 2019, and table 9 illustrates the estimated impacts on world price of alternative paths for stock changes by China. By delaying achievement of a 73-percent stocks-use ratio until 2023, world prices could be 13 percent higher during these years, and the discount necessary for reserve sales would only be 33

---

[23]Handpicked cotton usually has less plant matter (e.g., leaf particles) than mechanically harvested cotton, but often acquires contaminating fibers from harvesting sacks, clothing, and other household sources. Such contamination can be avoided, and the International Textile Manufacturers Federation's (ITMF) biannual surveys of reported contamination cite handpicked cotton from C-4 countries as among the world's least contaminated (ITMF, 2014).

[24]Exports before China's WTO accession had at times been subsidized and some subsidized exports continued in the period immediately after accession.

percent. Alternatively, if China reached a 40-percent stocks-use ratio in 2019, world prices would be 7 percent lower and the discount on China's reserve sales would exceed 50 percent. Note that raising support for prices above historical levels would also potentially reduce the discounts necessary to equate reserve sale prices and domestic market prices, but the resulting contraction in cotton consumption by China's textile mills would result in a reduction in their purchases from the reserve, postponing the adjustment costs by keeping the reserve large.

Table 9
Average price changes for alternative scenarios of China cotton endings stocks-use (SU) ratios compared with baseline[1]

Alternative 2019 SU ratio	Price change[2]	Alternative year to reach 73-percent SU ratio	Price change[3]
Percent		*Year*	*Percent*
40	-6.8	2017	-12.9
50	-4.8	2018	-5.3
60	-2.7	2019	0.0
70	-0.6	2020	4.1
80	1.5	2021	7.4
90	3.5	2022	10.2
100	5.6	2023	12.6

Notes: [1]Stocks- ratio for 2019 in 2014 USDA baseline is 73 percent. [2]Price change is average of each year's changes from 2014 to 2019. [3]Price change is average of each year's changes from 2014 to the alternative year.
Source: USDA, Economic Research Service (ERS) using Country-Commodity Linked System (CCLS) simulations and USDA/ERS, 2014. A CCLS version calibrated to the 2015 USDA international projections is not yet available, but the projections for both years are similar and model responses are not expected to differ between model versions.

Estimated Price Impact of China's Cotton Stock Changes

Simulations using USDA's Country-Commodity Linked System (CCLS) were used to estimate the impact on world prices of alternative approaches to reducing China's stocks.[25] The simulation results allow us to demonstrate the possible price impacts of China either repeating its 1999-2004 pattern of stock reduction or achieving another mixture of a final stock level and number of years to reach that level. The first step was to use the CCLS to establish the relationship between world cotton prices and China's cotton imports. The second step was to link scenarios of future cotton ending stock levels in China with annual import levels, compare those potential import levels with 2011-13 imports, and calculate an estimated price impact of the change in imports. Hypothetical future stock levels were linked with import levels by deriving forecasts of multiyear averages of China's excess demand for cotton from the USDA *International Long-term Projections to 2023* (USDA/ERS, 2014), and calculating average level of imports for China consistent with both USDA's estimates of excess demand and hypothetical future levels of China's ending stocks. [26]

The relationship between world prices and China's imports was estimated by comparing two scenarios simulated using the CCLS. In one scenario, USDA's China cotton baseline was adjusted to produce an initial 1-million-ton decline in China's imports every year; in the other scenario, this initial decline was 50 percent larger, at 1.5 million tons. New CCLS solutions were derived for world cotton markets, capturing the adjustments in response of supply and demand for cotton in China and the rest of the world to these exogenous shocks and the adjustment in world prices.

In each scenario, the biggest adjustment comes as a decline in price: which falls 10.3 percent on average due to the 1-million-ton shock (table 10) and 15.7 percent due to the 1.5-million-ton shock (table 11). The feedback of these world price adjustments on China's imports is relatively small, and about 90 percent of the initial import shock remains once equilibrium has been reached in each scenario. Production and consumption outside of China each change by about 2 percent in the first scenario and 3 percent in the second.

The ratio between the alternative import shocks is 1.5, and the ratio of the alternative price responses ranges from 1.50 in the first year to 1.53 in the ninth year. The implication of this consistency is that the world cotton price responds nearly linearly to changes in China's imports within this range. We can therefore extrapolate these estimated price changes to find the impact of import changes smaller than 1 million tons and larger than 1.5 million tons, and estimate the impact of a wider range of import reduction scenarios.

If China repeats the 1999-2004 pattern of stock reduction after 2013, its stocks-use ratio in 2019 (6 years later) would be 50 percent, and stocks would be 8 million tons smaller. During 2014-19, average excess demand in China and average annual levels of stock reduction would permit imports to average about 1.7 million tons annually. This would be a 2.5-million-ton reduction from the

---

[25]CCLS is a large-scale dynamic partial equilibrium simulation system consisting of 43 country and regional models. Each country and region is modeled to reflect domestic and trade policies and institutional behavior, such as tariffs, subsidies, and tariff rate quotas. Production, consumption, imports, and exports are endogenous and depend on domestic and world prices, which are solved within the modeling system. Macroeconomic assumptions and projections are exogenous, based on USDA's 10-year agricultural projections (USDA/ERS, 2014).

[26] A version of the CCLS calibrated to the USDA long-term projections released in 2014 (USDA/ERS, 2014) was used for this analysis. A CCLS version calibrated to the 2015 USDA international projections is not yet available, but the projections for both years are similar and model responses are not expected to differ between model versions.

Table 10
Change from baseline due to exogenous China cotton import reduction of 1 million tons[1]

	China imports	World price	Production (non-Chinese)	Consumption (non-Chinese)
	Thousand tons	-----------------------Percent-----------------------		
2015	-859	-12.4	-0.3	2.7
2016	-915	-10.9	-2.5	2.2
2017	-910	-11.0	-2.5	2.2
2018	-917	-10.6	-2.6	2.1
2019	-914	-10.3	-2.5	2.0
2020	-912	-10.0	-2.5	2.0
2021	-903	-9.6	-2.4	1.9
2022	-891	-9.2	-2.4	1.8
2023	-875	-8.9	-2.3	1.7
Average, 2015-2023	-899	-10.3	-2.2	2.1

[1]Production and consumption are endogenous in CCLS as well as prices. As a result, initial exogenous 1 million ton reductions in China's imports each year resulted in global equilibrium solutions in CCLS with less than 1-million-ton reductions in Chinese imports each year.
Source: USDA, Economic Research Service simulation using USDA/ERS Country-Commodity Linked System (CCLS), generated using the 2014 USDA baseline. A CCLS version calibrated to the 2015 USDA international projections is not yet available, but the projections for both years are similar and model responses are not expected to differ between model versions.

Table 11
Change from baseline due to exogenous China cotton import reduction of 1.5 million tons[1]

	China imports	World price	Production (non-Chinese)	Consumption (non-Chinese)
	Thousand tons	-----------------------Percent-----------------------		
2015	-1,288	-18.6	-0.5	4.1
2016	-1,375	-16.6	-3.7	3.3
2017	-1,367	-16.6	-3.8	3.3
2018	-1,379	-16.1	-3.9	3.1
2019	-1,378	-15.6	-3.8	3.0
2020	-1,374	-15.2	-3.8	2.9
2021	-1,357	-14.6	-3.7	2.8
2022	-1,336	-14.1	-3.6	2.6
2023	-1,312	-13.6	-3.5	2.5
Average, 2015-2023	-1,352	-15.7	-3.4	3.1

[1]Production and consumption are endogenous in CCLS as well as prices. As a result, initial exogenous 1 million ton reductions in China's imports each year resulted in global equilibrium solutions in CCLS with less than 1-million-ton reductions in Chinese imports each year.
Source: USDA, Economic Research Service simulation using USDA/ERS Country-Commodity Linked System (CCLS), generated using the 2014 USDA baseline. A CCLS version calibrated to the 2015 USDA international projections is not yet available, but the projections for both years are similar and model responses are not expected to differ between model versions.

average level of imports in 2011-13, and CCLS simulations suggest a sustained reduction in China's imports of this magnitude would reduce the world price of cotton by about 30 percent. Alternative patterns of stock reduction imply alternative levels of imports and greater or smaller price impacts: If the return to China's longrun stocks-use level of 50 percent is delayed until 2023, imports are higher and the price impact diminishes to a decline of slightly more than 15 percent. If stocks decline less—to an 80-percent stocks-use ratio—the price impacts of reaching that level in 2019 versus 2023 are declines of about 25 percent and 15 percent.

Three characteristics of the above estimates bear consideration. One is that the estimates are not forecasts but measures of the impact of one of numerous factors expected to affect future cotton prices.[27] A second is that the estimates are averages for the years between 2013 and the chosen year—the same level of imports is assumed for each year, but considerable annual variation would likely occur in actuality. The third characteristic is that each estimate describes only the price impact through the chosen year. In later years, once policies driving stock reduction are no longer being pursued and stocks-use can stabilize, annual excess demand would no longer be offset by falling stocks and imports would rise.

---

[27]USDA's 2015 baseline projections include a 22 percent decline in the U.S. upland cotton farm price during 2014-19 compared with 2011-13.

Conclusion

China's cotton policy during 2011-13 had unintended consequences and became unsustainable as an approach to support China's cotton producers, and China has seen its consumption of raw cotton drop sharply. China's policymakers have signaled their intentions to alter their cotton support to reduce the link between income and price support. There will be a period of transition as a more sustainable set of policies evolve and the policies will differ from those of the United States, reflecting the characteristics of China's agriculture and cotton industry. These new longrun policies and the policies of the transitional period will be designed to meet a set of goals, which include:

- sustaining a domestic cotton industry (particularly in Xinjiang) by offsetting the impact of rising wages on the production of a labor-intensive crop

- providing China's cotton yarn producers with access to relatively competitively-priced cotton

- efficiently using the share of government resources available to support agriculture

- directing the development of China's agricultural and industrial sectors to modernize, improve applied technology and value-added per unit of labor, and develop of large, integrated enterprises

China's agricultural support for cotton is expected to shift from a nearly complete reliance on price supports to a much greater reliance on income subsidies to farmers, utilizing a target-price-based system of payments to farmers to offset the impact of lower prices. China's ambitious goals for agricultural modernization are one reason for the decision to make Xinjiang the location for a pilot of this program—Xinjiang's farms are larger than those in other provinces, more highly mechanized, and their production system can be more readily integrated into China's modernized system of cotton quality management through machine classing (HVI). The full extension of this pilot to other provinces could be significantly influenced by policies to increase the scale of farming in China, directing subsidies to cooperatives and farms created by consolidating a large number of smaller plots.[28] Depending on the balance between the priorities of supporting current farmers and accelerating farm consolidation and modernization, cotton production in eastern China could fall significantly during a transitional period, but a significant reduction in imports would still be necessary to reduce stocks.

Sales from China's national cotton reserve will likely occur at discounts of 33-50 percent from the prices paid to purchase the cotton during 2011-13. The pace of these sales will be one factor determining the size of these discounts, due to the inverse relationship between the need for imports and the availability of cotton released from stocks, and the negative effect of lower imports by China on world cotton prices. Industry sources report that policy-makers in China are concerned about the implications of their new cotton policies for China's obligations as a member of the WTO—that too large a gap between the target price and market prices in Xinjiang could introduce, "the risk of the subsidy policy breaking WTO limitations of government subsidies."[29] China's WTO accession agreement limits support to 8.5 percent of the value of production, equivalent to less than $2

---

[28]The 2013 No. 1 Document of the CPC Central Committee laid out a program of reforming the management of property rights for farmers, facilitating the transfer from rural to urban residence registration for perhaps 100 million farmers, encouraging farmers to trade their rights to use farmland to individuals and entities that consolidate and directing subsidies to large-scale farming (Xinhuanet, 2013).

[29]*Cotton Outlook*, Vol. 92 No. 32, August 8, 2014.

billion each year for cotton during 2011-13. Since ICAC estimated the cost of maintaining China's 2013 national cotton reserve at $2 billion annually, China will face difficult choices as it seeks to limit expenditures for storage, while limiting the size of the discounts it accepts on reserve sales, and limiting the size of its target-price based subsidies.[30] Significant uncertainty remains about how China will deal with the unprecedented level of stocks accumulated during its 2011-13 price support effort, but a period of falling ending stock levels and lower imports by China is highly likely over several years.

---

[30]Gale (2013) noted that China appeared to have exceeded its product-specific de minimis level for cotton in 2011 and 2012 through its price support operations. With 2013 intervention purchases only 3 percent smaller than in 2012, and the support price unchanged, this appears to have been true in 2013 as well.

References

Alpermann, Bjorn. 2010. *China's Cotton Industry: Economic Transformation and State Capacity*, New York: Routledge

Amiti, Mary, and Caroline Fruend. 2010. "The Anatomy of China's Export Growth," in *China's Growing Role in World Trade*, Robert Feenstra and Shang-Jine Wei (eds.), University of Chicago Press.

Anderson, Kym, Marianne Kurzweil, Will Martin, Damiano Sandri, and Ernesto Valenzuela. 2008. "Measuring distortions to agricultural incentives, revisited," *World Trade Review*, 7(4): 675-704.

Beijing Zhongguo Jingji Daobao Online, June 25, 2014, translation by Open Source Center.

Beijing Cotton Outlook. 2014. CCIndex Database.

Brandt, Loren, Thomas Rawski, and John Sutton. 2008. "China's Industrial Development," in *China's Great Economic Transformation*, (Loren Brandt and Thomas G. Rawski (eds.), Cambridge University Press

Carter, Colin, Zhong Funing, and Jing Zhui. 2012. "Advances in Chinese Agriculture and its Global Implications," *Applied Economic Perspectives and Policy*, 34(1): 1-36.

Colby, Hunter, Frederick Crook, and Shu-Eng Webb. 1992. *Agricultural Statistics of the People's Republic of China, 1949-90,* U.S. Department of Agriculture, Economic Research Service, SB-844.

Cotlook Ltd., *Cotton Outlook*, various issues.

De Gorter, Harry, and Jana Hranaiova. 2004. "Quota Administration Methods: Economics and Effects with Trade Liberalization," in *Agriculture and the WTO: Creating a Trading System for Development*, Melinda Ingo and John Nash (ed.), World Bank.

Du, Min. 2011. *Investigation and Analysis on Production and Market Behavior of Cotton Growers in China*, presentation at 2011 China International Cotton Conference, Dalian, China, June 15-15, 2011.

Effland, Anne. 2011. *Classifying and Measuring Agricultural Support: Identifying Differences Between the WTO and OECD Systems*, U.S. Department of Agriculture, Economic Research Service, EIB-74. http://www.ers.usda.gov/publications/eib-economic-information-bulletin/eib74.aspx

Feike, Til, Yusuyunjiang Mamititmin, Lin Li, and Reiner Dolushitz. 2015. "Development of agricultural land and water use and its driving forces along the Aksu and Tarim River, P.R. China," *Environmental Earth Sciences*, 73(2), pp. 517-31.

Gale, Fred. 2013. *Growth and Evolution in China's Agricultural Support Policies*, U.S. Department of Agriculture, Economic Research Service, ERR-153. http://www.ers.usda.gov/publications/err-economic-research-report/err153.aspx

Food and Agriculture Organization of the United Nations and International Cotton Advisory Committee. 2013. *World Apparel Fiber Consumption Survey*.

Gale, Fred, and Robert Collender. 2006. *New Directions in China's Agricultural Lending*, U.S. Department of Agriculture, Economic Research Service, WRS-06-01.

Ge, Yuanlong, Holly Wang, and Sung Ahn. 2010. "Cotton market integration and the impact of China's new exchange rate regime," *Agricultural Economics*, 41(5): 443-451.

Global Trade Information Services. 2014. Global Trade Atlas.

Hua, Lui. 2013. *Thoughts of the Implementation of Macro Regulatory Policy for Cotton and CNCRC's Development Strategy*, presentation at Dialog on China's Cotton and Textile Industry Evolution, New York, July 15, 2013.

Hogg, Chris. 2010. "China Restores Xinjiang Internet," BBC News, May 14, 2010.

Huang, Jikun, Xiaobing Wang, and Scott Rozelle. 2013. "The subsidization of farming households in China's agriculture," *Food Policy* (41): 124-132.

InterContinental Exchange. 2014. *Cotton: Historical Prices*.

International Cotton Advisory Committee. 2013. *Production and Trade Policies Affecting the Cotton Industry*.

International Cotton Advisory Committee. *Review of the World Cotton Situation*, various issues.

International Monetary Fund. 2014a. International Financial Statistics.

International Monetary Fund. 2014b. IMF Primary Commodity Prices.

International Textile Manufacturers Federation. 2014. *Cotton Contamination Surveys (2003, 2005, 2007, 2009, 2011, 2013)*.

Jernigan, Ed. 2005. *Zhengzhou Cotton Futures: A Chinese Success Story*, presesntation at U.S. Department of Agriculture Agricultural Outlook Forum, February 25, 2005.

Kwiecinski, Andrzej, and Florence Broussard, 2013. *China: Estimates of Support to Agriculture*, Organization for Economic Cooperation and Development.

Krueger, Anne. 1974. "The political economy of the rent-seeking society," American Economic Review, 64(3): 291-303.

Meng, Lei. 2012. "Can grain subsidies impede rural–urban migration in hinterland China? Evidence from field surveys,",*China Economic Review*, 23: 729-741.

National Bureau of Statistics (a), *China Statistical Yearbook*, various issues.

National Bureau of Statistics (b), *China Yearbook of Agricultural Price Survey*, various issues.

National Development and Reform Commission, *China agricultural production costs and returns compilation*, various issues, Beijing, China: China Statistical Press

Orenstein, D.E., L. Jiang, and S.P. Hamburg. 2011. "An elephant in the planning room: Political demography and its influence on sustainable land-use planning in drylands," *Journal of Arid Environments* (75): pp. 596-611.

Organization for Economic Cooperation and Development. 2013a. *Value-Added Trade Database.*

Organization for Economic Cooperation and Development. 2013b. *Producer and Consumer Support Estimates Database.*

Piao, S., P. Ciais, Y. Huang, Z. Shen, S. Peng, J. Li, L. Zhou, H. Liu, Y. Ma, Y. Ding, P. Friedlingstein, C. Liu, K. Tan, Y. Yu, T. Zhang, and Jingyun Fang. 2010. "The impacts of climate change on water resources and agriculture in China," *Nature*, 467(7311): 43-51.

Quark, Amy. 2014. *Global Rivalries: Standard Wars and the Transnational Cotton Trade.* University of Chicago Press.

Renmin Ribao Online. January 20, 2014. "Drafting Team Member Cites Highlights of Central Document No. 1 on Food Security, Food Safety."

Shi, Jianwei. 2000. *Cotton Policy Adjustment Starting from 1999*, presentation at 25th International Cotton Conference, Bremen, Germany, March 1-4, 2000.

Studwell, Joe. 2013. *How Asia Works: Success and Failure in the World's Most Dynamic Region*, New York: Grove Press.

Sun, Ruizhe. 2013. China's Textile Industry—Today and Tomorrow, presentation at International Textile Manufacturers Federation Annual Conference 2013, Bregenz, Austria, September 10, 2013.

U.S. Department of Agriculture, Economic Research Service. 2014. *International Long-Term Projections to 2023.* http://www.ers.usda.gov/data-products/international-baseline-data.aspx

U.S. Department of Agriculture, Foreign Agricultural Service. 2014a. China Cotton Imports by Administrative Category, 2002-13.

U.S. Department of Agriculture, Foreign Agricultural Service. 2014b. Global Agricultural Information Network, "China, People's Republic of: Cotton and Products Annual," GAIN Report Number CH4015.

U.S. Department of Agriculture, Foreign Agricultural Service. 2014c. *Production, Supply and Distribution Online.* http://apps.fas.usda.gov/psdonline/

U.S. Department of Agriculture, International Commodity Estimates Committee (Cotton). 2014a. China Reserve Stocks Estimates.

U.S. Department of Agriculture, International Commodity Estimates Committee (Cotton). 2014b. Xinjiang Cotton Production, Area, and Yield Estimates.

U.S. Department of Agriculture, Office of the Chief Economist. 2015. *USDA Agricultural Projections to 2024, Long-term Projections*, OCE-2015-1. http://www.usda.gov/oce/commodity/projections/index.htm

U.S. Department of Agriculture, World Agricultural Outlook Board. 2014. *World Agricultural Supply and Demand Estimates*, WASDE-530. http://usda.mannlib.cornell.edu/usda/waob/wasde//2010s/2014/wasde-06-11-2014.pdf

Wang, Zhi, and and Shang-Jin Wei. 2008. *What accounts for the rising sophistication of China's exports?*, Working Paper 13771, National Bureau of Economic Research.

World Bank. 2007. *Distortions to Agricultural Incentives Database: China.*

World Trade Organization, Trade Policy Review Body. 2012. *Trade Policy Review, Report by the Secretariat: China.* WT/TPR/S/264.

World Trade Organization. 2014. *Statistics Database: Time Series on International Trade.*

Xinhuanet. 2013. "Xinhua Insight: Rural Reform, Step By Step" November 16, 2013.

Zhenzhou Commodity Exchange. 2014. *Historical Data: Cotton No. 1 Futures Contract.*

Zhu, Lanfen. 2001. *The Achievements and Prospects of China's Cotton Textile Industry*, presentation at 2001 China International Cotton Conference: Prospects of the World Cotton Market and the Chinese Cotton Industry in the New Millennium, Guilin, China, June 27-29, 2001, pp, 136-146.

Zhu, Ling. 2011. "Food Security and Agricultural Changes in the Course of China's Urbanization," *China and World Economy* 19(2): 40-59.